F

To Ryan and Tyler Brett

A NOTE FROM THE AUTHOR

In his *Book of Woodcraft* the great naturalist Ernest Thompson Seton listed forty birds that he thought every child should know. Though I disagreed with some of his selections, the listing made me think: How many and which birds should every child know? Which fish? Which mammals? What other animals?

The four books in the series CRINKLEROOT'S 100 ANIMALS EVERY CHILD SHOULD KNOW (*Crinkleroot's 25 Birds, 25 Fish, 25 Mammals*, and *25 More Animals*) are intended to provide a base of knowledge of the animal kingdom. I hope my selections will make parents and teachers consider, as Mr. Seton's forty birds made me consider, which other animals should be included.

—Jim Arnosky

Bradbury Press
Macmillan Publishing Company
866 Third Avenue
New York, NY 10022

Maxwell Macmillan Canada, Inc.
1200 Eglinton Avenue East
Suite 200
Don Mills, Ontario M3C 3N1

Macmillan Publishing Company is part of the
Maxwell Communication Group of Companies.

First edition
Printed and bound in the United States of America
10 9 8 7 6 5 4 3 2 1
The text is set in ITC Bookman Light. Typography by Julie Quan

Printed on recycled paper

LIBRARY OF CONGRESS CATALOGING-IN-PUBLICATION DATA
Arnosky, Jim.
Crinkleroot's 25 fish every child should know / by Jim Arnosky.
p. cm.
Summary: Presents paintings of twelve freshwater fish, including the carp, bass, and trout, and thirteen saltwater fish, including the flounder, tuna, swordfish and seahorse.
ISBN 0-02-705844-1
1. Fishes—Juvenile literature.   2. Fishes—Identification—Juvenile literature. [1. Fishes.   2. Freshwater fishes.
3. Marine fishes.]   I. Title.   II. Title: Crinkleroot's twenty-five fish every child should know.   III. Title: 25 fish every child should know.
QL617.2.A76   1993
597—dc20   92-39381

Crinkleroot's
25 FISH
EVERY CHILD SHOULD KNOW

BY JIM ARNOSKY

BRADBURY PRESS   NEW YORK

Maxwell Macmillan Canada   Toronto
Maxwell Macmillan International
New York   Oxford   Singapore   Sydney

GILL

Hello! My name is Crinkleroot. I'm a friend to all the animals. How many animals do you know?

In this book, there are twenty-five fish you should know.

Fish live in water. They can breathe underwater because they have gills.

Fish swim by flexing their strong backbones
and waving their fins.

Some fish leap into the air and splash
back down. They dart and dash.
They sparkle and flash.

Some fish move
slowly, like shadows
in the water.

Certain kinds of fish live in fresh water, while other
kinds live in salt water. The first twelve fish
in this book are found in fresh water.
The next thirteen are saltwater fish.

Have fun learning your fish!

Your friend, *Crinkleroot*

Goldfish

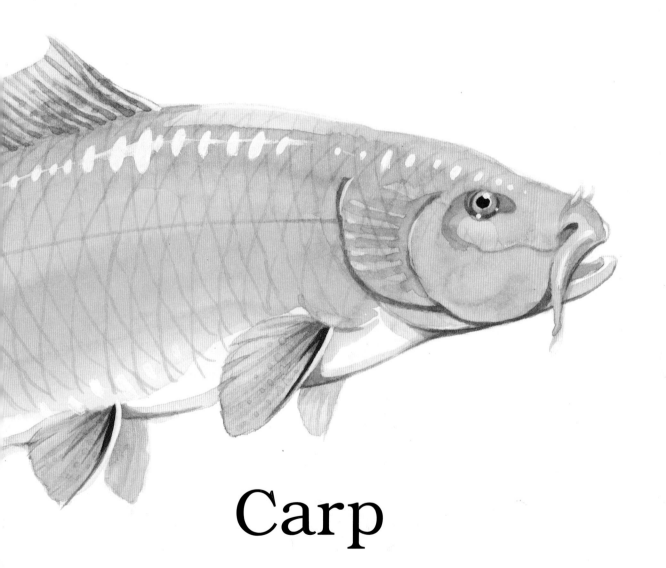

Carp

Sunfish

Bass

Perch

Trout

Minnow

Sucker

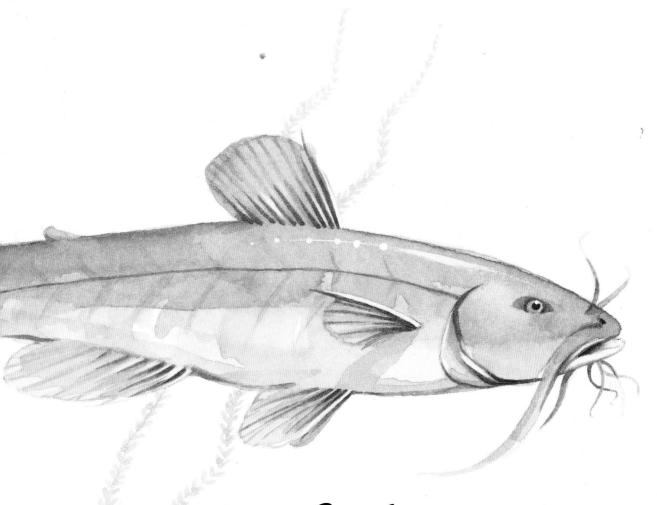

Catfish

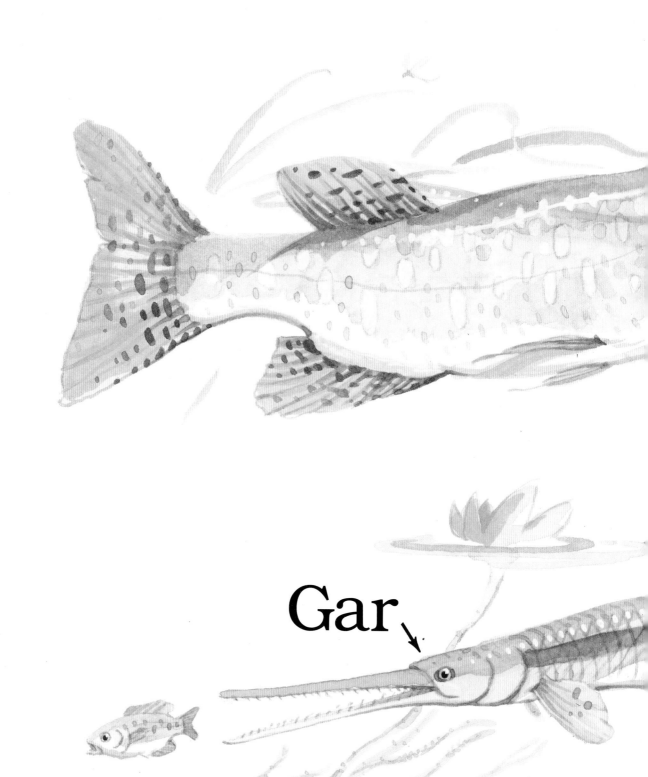

Gar

Pike

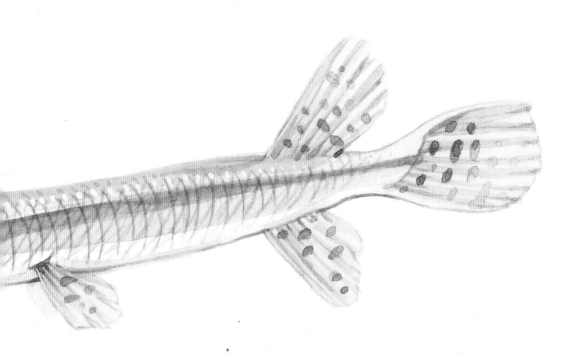

Eel

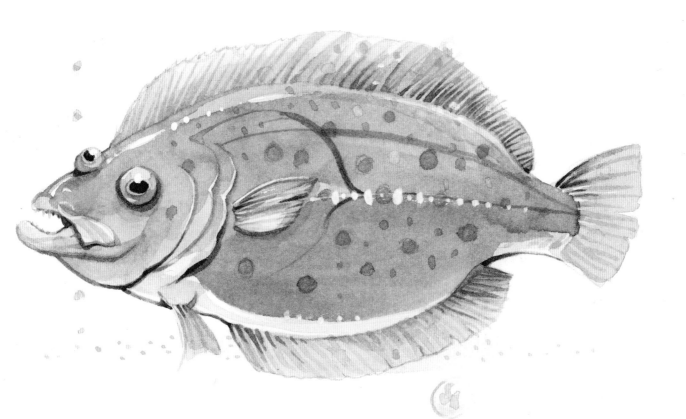

Flounder

Herring

Cod

Mackerel

Barracuda

Bluefish

Tuna

Swordfish

Stingray

Shark

Flying Fish

Angelfish

Sea Horse